Introduction To

CIVIL WAR
PHOTOGRAPHY

Ross J. Kelbaugh

JEFF DAVIS 'taking' WASHINGTON.

Woodcut from a Northern patriotic envelope.

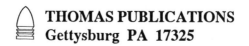

THOMAS PUBLICATIONS
Gettysburg PA 17325

Copyright © 1991 Ross J. Kelbaugh

Printed in the United States of America

Published by THOMAS PUBLICATIONS
        P.O. Box 3031
        Gettysburg PA 17325

ISBN-0-939631-36-9

CONTENTS

This photograph of Antietam is one of the most famous images taken during the Civil War and among the first to ever document the grim face of battle. It is reproduced from one side of the wet-plate stereo negatives taken by Alexander Gardner who was working for Mathew Brady.

PREFACE

Most Americans first encounter Civil War photographs printed in their grade school history textbooks. Unfortunately, authors rarely discuss the various types of pictures copied to make these illustrations or even explain just how the originals were made. Few photographers other than Mathew Brady are ever mentioned giving the inaccurate impression that he alone was responsible for all of the images of the war. Many families have inherited photographs of ancestors that participated in this event, but they often know little about their heirlooms. These artifacts have also received increased attention among those who collect the relics of this era.

Though the number of books about the war continues to grow, few provide a non-technical introduction to photography of the period.

This publication is written for the general audience interested in early photography who would like to learn more about the images of this dynamic era. For the Civil War enthusiast, you will get a better understanding of how these pictures were produced. For the caretaker of the family archives, you will get a better idea about how to interpret your ancestor's visual legacy. For the budding collector, you will gain valuable guidance that will help you enter this growing collecting field.

I obtained my first photographs of Civil War soldiers while in the seventh grade during the Civil War Centennial. In recent years, part of my collecting and research has focused on uncovering photography's story in my home state of Maryland. Many of this book's illustrations and stories are the result of this work and are published here for the first time. Though some of the focus is local, the story is national. The practice of photography was fairly standardized throughout the country. However, Baltimore, the city of divided loyalties, held a unique position during the war which helped make its long forgotten photographic story particularly interesting today.

I would like to thank Henry Deeks, Herb Peck, and Bill Simmermacher for sharing images from their extensive collections. Unless otherwise noted, photographs used for illustrations are my own treasures.

Among these pages, I share some of what I have learned as part of my own adventure of discovery. I hope this serves as a valuable guide to accompany you on your journey into the past.

Ross J. Kelbaugh
Baltimore, Maryland

An unidentified Union soldier, wearing the distinctive uniform of Collis' Zouaves, was photographed by B.F. Reimer in Philadelphia at the beginning of the Civil War. The original albumen print, the source for this illustration, was bought at a Maryland flea market for just a few dollars.

INTRODUCTION

Of all the events in American history, one continues to stand out above all others - the Civil War. Though the participants are long since gone, their story still captures our national imagination. Books, magazines, and movies continue to chronicle their exploits. Tourists visit the battlefields to view for themselves the setting for this drama. Volunteers recreate the era through battle reenactments and living history demonstrations. Collectors compete for Civil War relics. Though this event occurred so long ago, why has interest in it endured? The answer to this is due, in part, to the miracle of an invention that arrived little more than twenty years before the war - photography. The Civil War was the first conflict in history to be so extensively recorded. We are still able to look upon the faces of the famous and forgotten. We can see the places where they made history almost as if we are looking through their eyes. For us today, photography is the key to unlocking the door to this part of our past.

Photography was little more than two decades old before the cannons sounded at Fort Sumter on April 12, 1861. In 1839, Louis Daguerre announced in France that he had achieved what many had thought impossible - capturing reality in its most minute detail on a polished silver plate. This new invention, named the daguerreotype after its discoverer, quickly captivated the world.

But the daguerreotype was not destined to be part of the story of the Civil War. Following on the heels of the French discovery, an Englishman, William Henry Fox Talbot, revealed his own photographic invention - the Talbotype or Calotype. This technique, which used "negatives" to print images on paper, laid the foundation for another process that served as the basis for photography during the Civil War.

In 1851, Frederick Scott Archer demonstrated a photographic method that was built upon the earlier invention of his fellow countryman, Fox Talbot. Archer had searched for a medium to replace Talbot's paper negatives. Prints from these never captured the clarity and detail reproduced by the daguerreotype, which had accounted for the initial popularity of the French invention. Archer experimented with using sheets of glass as the base for the light sensitive chemicals. The problem was how to keep this solution from running off while the plate was exposed in a camera. Archer came up with the idea of first coating it with a transparent liquid called "collodion" (from a Greek word meaning "to stick") that adhered to the glass. Once the plate was coated, a bath in a solution of silver nitrate made it light sensitive, but only while the chemicals remained tacky or wet. Collodion or "wet-plate" photography was born.

By the mid-1850s, this new photographic process began to eclipse the daguerreotype in America. (Few daguerreotypes dating from the Civil War are known to exist today.) As the South departed from the Union after the election of Abraham Lincoln in 1860, wet-plate photography stood ready to record the actors and scenery of this national drama.

Phillips & Frear of New York, recorded in this carte de visite, were among the thousands of photographers working in the United States during the Civil War. The partner on the left posed holding his watch which he used to time the length of the exposure of the wet-plate negative inside the camera.

THE PHOTOGRAPHERS

Due to the complex nature of the technology, the practice of photography was generally limited to the professional during most of the nineteenth century. More than three thousand photographers have been documented to have worked in the medium throughout the United States during the Civil War. Most were male, although many women operated their own studios. Several free African-Americans owned galleries in both the North and the South. Some added an additional sideline to supplement their earnings in photography - particulary if they worked in areas with small numbers of likely patrons. Though few got wealthy, the possibility of a modest living as independent businessmen made the occupation attractive to many.

Photography was no more difficult to master than other trades that demanded special skills and training. A person desiring to enter the field could apprentice in a studio to learn the wet-plate process. Some veteran cameramen offered lessons for a fee which included the equipment needed to start a business. Manuals describing the details of the various processes were widely circulated throughout the country. Photographic supplies were usually available in larger cities. Anyone with the determination and a modest amount of capital could start making pictures. Consequently, those seeking to immortalize themselves in a photograph often had several studios of varying quality and price from which to choose. Competition, particularly in the larger towns and cities, was keen, and the life of many studios was often brief.

Starting in September 1862, the trade faced additional expenses. All professional photographers in the United States were required to purchase an annual license as part of a federal program designed to raise money to support the war effort. Licenses cost either $10, $15, or $25 depending on the amount of business done during a year. As territory of the rebellious states was occupied by Union forces, photographers operating in those areas were subject to the tax as well. By April 1863, Southern photographers had to pay the Confederate government an annual fee of $50 and 2 1/2% tax on total sales.

The Civil War presented a unique opportunity for the more adventurous in the picture trade. Itinerant photographers had traveled throughout the nation before the war to take the magic of their medium to America's small towns and countryside. The armies of the North, the largest ever seen in the nation's history, presented an extraordinary business opportunity. As soldiers joined their forces, they often found photographers set up near their camps and winter quarters plying their services to recruits and veterans alike. There was little reason for a Union soldier's family to be without his photograph as scores of photographers followed the armies of blue.

Confederate soldiers, however, were not quite so fortunate. Wartime shortages brought on by the ever tightening noose of the blockade made photography in the South increasingly difficult. Chemicals and plates became in short supply, though most Southern cities had galleries in operation throughout the war. Some Northern photographers and supply houses helped smuggle materials through to their counterparts below the Mason-Dixon line so their work could continue. A few Southerners recorded views of Confederate forts and encampments to sell to supporters of the Cause. Others visited the armies in the field to offer their portrait service, and some maintained small town studios despite the obstacles. But photographic activities within the seceded states remained much more limited than those in the North during the war. This accounts today for the relative rarity of photographs made in the Confederacy.

THE BOY HAS HIS PICTURE TAKEN.

This print records a scene familiar to many Civil War soldiers. While the photographer exposed the plate inside the camera, the young subject was steadied by the headstand. Note the skylight which provided the natural illumination required in the days before use of an artificial flash.

THE PHOTOGRAPHER'S STUDIO

When Johnny Reb and Billy Yank marched off to war, most wanted to leave behind a lasting memento of themselves for family and friends. The thousands of photography studios spread throughout the country recorded many of the portraits of the Civil War soldiers that still exist today. They ranged from simple one-room establishments in small towns, to the large city galleries (such as those of Mathew Brady in New York and Washington, D.C.) with large waiting rooms decorated in the latest Victorian decor. When soldiers arrived in camp, they found itinerant photographers operating from special tents, wagons, and primitive cabins as well.

All of these professionals, whose stories have often been lost in time, provided future generations with the first extensive recording of participants in an American war.

Photographers during this period faced numerous technical limitations. A nearby darkroom was needed to prepare and develop the glass plates used in the collodion process. An adequate source of natural light, either from a glass skylight or an opening in a tent roof, provided the illumination needed to take a picture in the era before the artificial flash. The time allowed for exposing the light sensitive plate in the camera was measured in seconds. Subjects were required to hold a still pose steadied by an iron headclamp on a stand poised behind them. (This is why there are no photographs of Civil War battles.) In spite of these and other difficulties, photographers of this era created a remarkable visual legacy.

For those desiring a "likeness," the procedures were fairly routine. The soldier, often having been attracted by trade signs and a display of the photographer's work outside the studio, entered into a reception area inside. There he was greeted by the proprietor or an assistant who explained the types and sizes of photographs offered and their costs. After a selection was made, the customer waited to be called for his sitting.

The soldier was led into the studio once it was prepared. Across from the camera perched on a stand often sat a posing chair and table in front of a canvas backdrop. The canvas may have been painted to resemble an outdoor scene containing cannons, tents, and flags, or it may have been left plain. The headclamp or "iron instrument of torture" was positioned behind the subject, who probably sat or stood next to a small table, to steady his pose during the exposure. (More elaborate studio settings included columns and drapes as well.) As the roof skylight illuminated the room, the photographer adjusted a screen next to the scene to obtain just the right balance of light and shade. Attention now turned to the camera. This instrument, the most expensive piece of the photographer's equipment, was basically a light proof wooden box with a brass tube containing glass lenses attached to the front. The technical part of this process now commenced.

The photographer, with his head covered by a black cloth, viewed the scene from the back of his camera. As he peered at his patron before him, he adjusted the lens to focus the image reflected on a special glass before his eyes. After making any last minute changes to the subject and/or setting, the photographer retrieved from his workroom the sensitized glass negative held inside a light proof wooden carrier. (To speed up the process, an assistant would have prepared the plate while the studio arrangements were made.) After removing the focusing glass from the back of the camera, the plate carrier was slipped in. A slide was pulled away so the plate could be exposed in the camera. Now one of the most critical steps occurred.

According to the standards of the day, a successful photograph was more than a mere recording of a person. It also tried to capture their "spirit" through their expression. (Unfortunately, many photographers never progressed beyond making only "likenesses.") As the artist conversed with his sitter, he waited for just the right look. At that moment, the subject was told to hold the pose as a cap on the camera lens was removed. A pocket watch and experience helped judge the length of the exposure that might last for as long as ten seconds. When enough light had entered to expose the plate, the cap was placed back over the lens. As the subject was led from the studio, the plate, still in its light proof carrier, was taken back to the workroom to be developed and fixed (made insensitive to light).

Depending on the type ordered, the finished photograph could be ready within the hour or not until the following day. After viewing his portrait, the soldier selected a proper case, if required, and was presented with a bill. In the more expensive city galleries, customers were not usually charged until they were satisfied with the results. ("Cheap" studios often required payment first.) After settling his account, the patriot then departed with his precious package to be shared with family, friends, and posterity.

Traveling photographers' Engle & Furlong made a carte de visite of their specially designed studio tent. The opening in the roof was for the skylight. Courtesy Henry Deeks.

An unidentified Yankee soldier stood upon muddy ground for his quarter plate tintype in the studio tent of a camp photographer. The next customer for the camera's lens peeks out from behind the canvas on the left.

Richard Walzl's advertising carte de visite displayed various types of photographs, albums, frames, and tools of the trade from the wet-plate era. Walzl was arrested early in the war on suspicions of disloyalty when he returned to the North after working briefly as a photographer in the Confederate capital.

Columns, drapes, and balustrades along with scenic backdrops, some with military themes, were among the popular props in city galleries. Settings in smaller town studios were often more simply composed.

Collodion glass plate negative processed to make an ambrotype. When backed with black material, the familiar positive image is created.

A thin brass mat and a protective sheet of glass were placed over the image. A brass edging called a preserver held the sandwich together.

The package was placed into a "miniature" case.

Sixth plate thermoplastic cases used to hold ambrotypes and tintypes. These patriotic designs were among the many styles that decorated those of the Civil War era.

THE AMBROTYPE

The first popular type of photograph made by the collodion process was called the "ambrotype," after a Greek word meaning "immortal." Its appearance resembled a daguerreotype except glass, instead of a silver plate, was used as the base for the image. This eliminated the reflections created by Daguerre's invention which made the picture difficult to see at certain angles. In addition, the plate could usually be finished so the image was not reversed (like your reflection in a mirror) without a special device inside the camera. The ambrotype quickly became popular with the public and its reign lasted from the mid-1850s through the early 1860s. Many Civil War soldiers chose this process to immortalize themselves for loved ones back home.

The ambrotype was basically a thin or light collodion negative on a glass plate. When backed with black varnish, paper, cloth or made on dark ruby colored glass, the negative turned into a positive photograph. Consequently, each ambrotype is unique since it is the actual plate that was exposed to light in the camera. To get a duplicate, the soldier had to either sit for another picture or have his original copied. Images were made in several sizes with the largest being the most expensive. These included the following:

> sixteenth plate - 1 3/8 x 1 5/8 inches
> ninth plate - 2 x 2 1/2 inches
> sixth plate - 2 3/4 x 3 1/4 inches
> quarter plate - 3 1/4 x 4 1/4 inches
> half plate - 4 1/4 x 5 1/2 inches
> whole plate - 6 1/2 x 8 1/2 inches

The sixth plate, about the size of an ordinary man's wallet, was the most popular choice in America.

Due to its fragile nature, the ambrotype was carefully packaged after the plate had been developed and finished by the photographer. First, a thin brass mat was placed over the image, followed by a protective cover glass. This sandwich was held together by a thin brass rim known as a "preserver." A miniature case was then selected to house this package. The image was slipped into the right half opposite a pad, usually of velvet, on the left. (Some, however, were made to hold photographs on both sides.) The cheapest examples were made of embossed paper applied over a wooden shell. Leather was used as a covering as well. A molded thermoplastic (sometimes incorrectly called "gutta-percha") "Union" case was the most expensive choice. A sixth plate in a leather case, the most common selection, cost about $1.50 - well within the means of Civil War officers and many enlisted men.

In some ambrotypes, the identities of the soldiers and/or galleries were included. Photographers sometimes stamped their names on the mat, embossed it on the pad inside the miniature case, or placed a tradecard behind the image. A few, like Richmond photographer Charles Rees, scratched their names on the plate in the collodion. Some mats may be stamped "Cutting's Pat. July 4 & 11, 1854." James Cutting, who held patents for collodion solutions and a method for sealing together the image plate and covering glass, sold licenses to photographers to use his processes. Soldiers may be identified by paper attached to the case pad of placed behind the image. Unfortunately, most ambrotypes are unsigned and the identities of subjects and photographers are unknown.

Sixth plate ambrotype of a Confederate who joined the Jackson Guard in Tennessee. Few cased images include such detailed identification as included here. This was purchased by the author at a shopping mall antique show. Courtesy Herb Peck, Jr.

The Virginia state seal on the belt plate worn by this Southern cavalryman makes his sixth plate ambrotype particularly collectible.

The cracked glass of this sixth plate ambrotype shows the fragile nature of this format.

Sixth plate ambrotype of a well armed Union infantryman wearing an upside down "VMM" (Volunteer Maine Militia) belt plate and holding an English Enfield rifle.

Quarter plate ambrotype of two Union artillerymen wearing "Hardee" style hats and holding Whitney (left) and Colt (right) revolvers. Courtesy Bill Simmermacher Collection.

Quarter plate ambrotype of a New England fifer wearing his recently issued equipment. Images of musicians are desirable among collectors.

Portrait of Baltimoreans James and John Kane who served under the famed Confederate Colonel John S. Mosby. The brothers struck this pose in the Bendann studio at the end of the war. Unfortunately, the original carte de visite copied here has since been lost.

THE CARTE DE VISITE

By the beginning of the Civil War, the wet-plate process had spawned another photographic format that soon replaced the ambrotype. Named the carte de visite (French for "visiting card"), it became the rage among soldiers and civilians in the United States during the 1860s and is the source for many portraits of Civil War personalities published today.

Like its cousin the ambrotype, the carte de visite was the product of a glass plate. Following the collodion process, the photographer first prepared and exposed his glass plate in his camera. A special combination of chemicals and exposure times produced a darker or thicker negative (unlike the thin negative for the ambrotype) on the plate when it was developed. Once fixed and dried, the real advantages over the ambrotype became apparent.

The creation of a glass negative made is possible for the photographer to make an unlimited number of paper prints. First, the glass negative was placed on top of photographic paper that had been made light sensitive with a bath in a solution of silver nitrate. The earliest photographic paper had been coated with salt which was followed by a sensitizing bath. The "salt print" was mostly employed just before and during the earliest years of the war. Paper coated with chicken egg albumen and salt was more common during the conflict. (Printing paper was difficult to make, but it could be purchased commercially prepared.) The negative and paper were exposed to daylight which caused a positive image to be printed out on the paper. Once the photographer was satisfied with it, the paper was fixed and given a bath in a toner. Then it was hung up to dry. The print could even be hand tinted by the photographer or a special "colorist." The use of the glass negative now made is possible to reproduce an unlimited number of copies from one negative. The question, though, was what size to make these paper prints?

In Victorian times, it was customary to leave calling cards when visiting friends and to exchange them with new acquaintances. These usually had the name of the bearer written or engraved in a stylish manner upon it. A French photographer to the court of Napoleon III, Adolph Disderi, had the idea that paper prints made from the collodion negative should be mounted on cardboard cut the size of these calling cards (about 2 1/2 inches by 4 inches), and the carte de visite was born. Special cameras with four lenses were eventually developed that enabled the photographer to make four separate negatives at one time on the same plate. This increased the number of images that could be contact printed from a single plate. Cartes de visite were usually purchased by the dozen at a cost of about $2.50 to $3.00.

By 1860, the carte de visite style had been adopted by many photographers in the United States, and citizens soon found themselves overwhelmed with the new paper photographs. As a result, the first photograph albums were introduced to house cartes de visite. These usually had embossed leather covers and contained pages designed to allow the insertion of card photographs. Soon no parlor was considered complete without the family album filled with the pictures of friends, family, and notables of the day.

Cartes de visite were made in America until the early 1880s. They were most popular, however, during the Civil War years, and there are several ways to identify those from this period. These images are usually recognized by their thin square cornered mounts which often have two thin gold lines printed along the edges. Unlike earlier photographs, many photographers often stamped or printed their names and the location of their studios on the front of the card below the print or on the back. This information can be helpful in dating a picture. Since many of these people moved around frequently or operated only a short time, directories of photographers now being published can be helpful in determining when studios were active at a particular location. Other pieces of evidence may also be present. From September 1, 1864, to August 1, 1866, photographs were among a number of articles that were taxed by the federal government to raise money for the war. A revenue stamp (its amount depended on the photograph's cost, but it was usually about 3 cents) was supposed to be applied to the back of the card. The photographer was also required to cancel the stamp and mark the date of the business transaction. Unfortunately, many only placed a slash or their initials upon it. Since cards were easy to write on, soldiers often signed their names and sometimes included their military unit as well. Copies of soldiers' military service records can be obtained from the National Archives or other sources. Careful study of a carte de visite can often reveal many clues that help in interpreting it today.

The carte de visite camera with four lenses enabled the photographer to make four or more exposures on the same plate at one time. International Museum of Photography, George Eastman House.

Embossed leather cover for a typical carte de visite album.

The photograph album contained pages designed so cards could be slipped in for display. Pictured is Union General Franz Sigel.

Carte De Visite (continued)

The ability to mass produce prints from a collodion negative also spawned a new industry. The public wanted to see the faces of the major characters in this national drama. The technology to mechanically reproduce photographs (as in this book) did not exist during that time, so photographers published cartes de visite of prominent personalities of the day. Photography studios and book and stationery stores sold photographs (made from engravings or life) of actors and actresses, politicians, military leaders, and other notable personages. Northerners inserted cartes of Lincoln, McClellan or Grant and Southerners added their Lee's, Stuart's, and Jackson's to the pages of the family album. The demand for cartes de visite of Confederate generals and statesmen was so strong in Union occupied Baltimore that the military command banned their sale in March 1863. This did not totally eliminate the trade in "contraband pictures," because young boys took to the streets to secretly market the illegal images to local Southern sympathizers.

Americans often posed with tools used in their occupations when having portraits taken during the nineteenth century. Each of the workers in this carte de visite demonstrated for the camera his role in the production of hardtack, a staple of the Civil War soldier's diet. Photographs of the industries that supplied the armies are uncommon.

After he received command of Virginia's troops, the Bendann Brothers published this carte de visite of Robert E. Lee at the beginning of the war. Private collection.

Confederate Colonel Roger Hanson had his portrait taken in Baltimore while held as a paroled prisoner waiting exchange. He was later killed in battle. Private collection.

This carte de visite copy of a highly retouched photograph of Confederate cavalryman J.E.B. Stuart is a less collectible portrait of a popular subject.

Carte de visite portrait of Charles Johnson, who served in the Second Maryland Artillery, C.S.A., was taken in 1862 after his discharge due to illness.

Carte de visite of a Union fifer from New York.

Carte de visite of an unidentified Union sailor. Images of African-American soldiers are scarce.

Lt. McGrath from New York was unusually relaxed for his carte de visite portrait. The identification and pose make this image very collectible. Private collection.

Reverse of a carte de visite showing the photographer's imprint and the canceled revenue stamp required from September 1, 1864 to August 1, 1866.

STEPS OF THE CARTE DE VISITE PROCESS

The following description of the extensive procedures followed by Civil War photographers to make a negative and print a photograph is adapted from *The Photography Manual* by N.G. Burgess published in 1863.

Making A Negative

1. Preparing the Gun Cotton - Soak clean fibers of cotton in a solution of sulphuric acid with nitric acid or nitrate of potash. The manufacture of gun-cotton is usually very difficult and dangerous. It is therefore recommended that it be purchased whenever possible.

2. Making Collodion - Mix gun-cotton with sulphuric ether and alcohol until the cotton dissolves. The collodion must be perfectly clear and transparent to work successfully.

3. Coating the Plate - Pour the collodion mixture from a bottle on to a carefully cleaned sheet of glass with a continuous stream until the whole surface is covered. Let the superfluous quantity run off at the right-hand edge into the bottle. Let the coating dry until it almost appears free from moisture.

4. Sensitizing the Plate - Darken the room; place the plate in a bath of iodide of silver for one to two minutes. After removing the plate, the solution on its surface should be uniform, clear, and without any lines or streaks.

5. Exposing the Plate - Enclose the glass in the plateholder and place it in the camera. Expose the plate by removing the cap on the lens. The time allowed is a matter of judgment and experience. In a strong light, and depending on the type of collodion used, fifteen seconds to one minute will be sufficient.

6. Developing the Negative - Remove the plate from its holder in the darkroom. Pour the developer (a solution of protosulphite of iron and acetic acid) over the coated side of the glass. After allowing the solution to remain on the surface for a few seconds, the outlines of the negative will appear. If it is not sufficiently intense, coat it again two or three more times.

7. Fixing the Negative - Thoroughly wash the plate with water and immerse the plate in a flat dish containing a strong solution of hyposulphite of soda. Once the plate has lost its milky appearance, wash again to remove the last traces of soda.

8. Varnishing the Negative - In order to preserve negatives for future use, it is well to varnish them. If they are intended only to print a few copies, a varnish of gum-arabic is preferable. If the negative is required for many prints, the better course would be to use the white negative varnish. All varnishes are poured over the plate in the manner of the collodion and allowed to dry by being placed on its edge in the plate stand. Once dry, the negative is ready for printing photographs.

The photographer coats a glass plate with collodion.

Preparing A Carte de Visite

1. Silvering (sensitizing) the Paper - Float a sheet of albumen paper face down in a solution of nitrate of silver dissolved in water for five minutes. Hang up the silvered paper in a dark room to dry.

2. Printing from the Negative - Place the glass negative on top of the sensitized paper in the printing frame. Expose to natural light until the desired image intensity is obtained. Remove the print from the frame in a darkroom.

3. Toning the Print - First wash the paper a in small quantity of water. Then lay it aside in another dish of water that is excluded from light. Then place the paper in another dish that holds equal parts of a gold (chloride of gold and water) and alkaline (bicarbonate of soda and water) solution. Keep the solution in motion until the desired tone is attained.

4. Fixing the Print - Wash the print in running water for fifteen to twenty minutes. Then bath it in a solution of hyposulphate of soda for fifteen to twenty minutes to produce a clear tone. The print should be well washed again and hung up to dry.

5. Mounting the Carte de Visite - Lay the print on a glass of the size desired and use a pair of scissors to trim it to the edges of the glass. Glue the print to the card using a gelatine or gum-arabic solution, mucilage, or a paste made from common starch. After the carte de visite is mounted and dried, it is much improved by running the card through a "photographic press" or rolling machine which renders it smoother and greatly improved by the process.

6. Coloring the Carte de Visite - Mix a preparation of gall with water-colors ordinarily used for photographs and apply with a fine brush. A slight varnishing will be required after coloring made of albumen or dextrine, carefully strained, and laid on with a flat brush.

Carte de visite portrait of a "colorist" who specialized in hand tinting photographs.

An uncased quarter plate tintype of a Union soldier holding another quarter plate image of two comrades. Could the soldiers in the picture have been friends fallen in battle? Unfortunately, their story has been lost in time.

THE TINTYPE

In 1856, another type of photograph using the wet-plate process was patented. Named the "melainotype" (from a Greek word meaning "black") or "ferrotype" (from Latin for "iron"), it became commonly known as the "tintype," although tin was actually never used in the process. These photographs became the most common form for inexpensive images made during the Civil War and are found bearing the pictures of both Northern and Southern soldiers.

A tintype was quite similar to its cousin, the ambrotype, but a few differences insured its success. Instead of coating a sheet of glass with collodion, the photographer substituted a blackened piece of sheet iron. Once the plate was sensitized, exposed, and developed, the photographic image appeared upon its surface. (With no intermediate negative, the image is reversed which makes numbers and letters appear backwards.) Since the black metal base rendered the picture as a positive, the backing techniques used with the ambrotype were not needed. The metal plate was also not as fragile as glass so a soldier's tintype could be easily sent through the mail. Though the image did not duplicate the tonal range found in the ambrotype, the cheap cost made it very popular, especially with the lower paid enlisted men of the Union army. Confederate tintypes, however, became less common as the war progressed due to the increasing scarcity of sheet metal.

Tintypes were usually packaged in several ways. Initially, photographers offered them in the same sizes and cased like ambrotypes. (Sometimes a cased image has to be carefully studied to identify the exact process used to make it.) To lower their cost, special cameras were designed to make multiple exposures on one plate. These were snipped apart after processing. Carte de visite size tintypes were placed in a special miniature case or in a paper sleeve that had a cutout which framed the image on the front and usually carried the photographer's business imprint on the reverse. During the latter years of the war, "gem pictures" became popular. These tintypes, about 1 inch by 1 inch in size or smaller, were mounted on or inside a carte de visite size paper sleeve and sold for as little as four for 25 cents. Family albums from the Civil War era often contain tintypes as well as cartes de visite among its pages.

Several techniques can be used to date a tintype. Plates of the war period sometimes have their edges stamped "Melainotype Plate/For Neffs Pat/19 Feb 56" or "Griswold's Pat. Melainotype." Peter Neff had bought the patent rights to the ferrotype from its inventor, Professor Hamilton Smith, and sold his process throughout the country along with a license to make the thin iron sheets. Victor Griswold also manufactured his brand of "ferrotype plates." Like the ambrotype, soldiers sometimes wrote their names in the miniature cases and photographers occasionally included tradecards behind the image, but many are unidentified. Names of soldiers are often found written on the paper sleeves holding their tintype, and the photographer's imprint is stamped on the back. Research of the subject's military records and photographer directories may help in narrowing the time period of the image. Like cartes de visite, tintypes were also subject to the special 1864-1866 tax and the presence of a revenue stamp gives additional clues for dating.

This sixth plate tintype of a Confederate cavalryman was purchased by the author early in the morning at the famed Brimfield flea markets in Massachusetts. The soldier's "CSA" belt plate and Smith carbine make this a particularly desirable image for collectors.

Uncased sixth plate tintype of a Union sergeant holding a noncommissioned officer's sword. Courtesy Bill McIntosh.

Ninth plate tintype of a Union soldier wearing his overcoat and holding a belt knife and Colt Model 1849 pocket revolver. Courtesy Bill Simmermacher Collection.

Ninth plate tintype of John Thomas Gregg taken December 4, 1863. Unfortunately, it is unusual to find such an informative label placed inside a case.

Carte de visite portrait of Daniel (seated) and David (standing) Bendann. The brothers had the rare opportunity of photographing both Union and Confederate soldiers, and many of their cartes de visite survive today. Private collection.

THE BENDANNS OF BALTIMORE

Baltimore, Maryland, held a unique position among Northern cities during the Civil War. As the fourth largest in the Union, the population was further increased by the regiments of troops stationed in the forts that ringed the city of divided loyalties. Its railroads and harbor funneled soldiers (including paroled Confederate officers) south to the nation's capital and beyond. Since May 1861, the city was ruled by martial law and even the suspicion of disloyalty could result in imprisonment. Public displays of Southern symbols were quickly outlawed, and the sale of photographs of Confederate soldiers and statesmen was banned in March 1863. Within this climate, almost fifty photographic studios offered their services to those desiring to have a likeness taken; there was a photographer to serve every size wallet. Among the expensive "artistic" studios, the gallery of David and Daniel Bendann ranked among the best.

The Bendann Gallery was opened at 205 Baltimore Street in 1859, after the brothers located there from Richmond, Virginia. They were soon known for the technical and artistic quality of their work and were among the first to offer the carte de visite to Baltimore. When the war commenced, the brothers used negatives and photographs obtained while working in Richmond to publish a series of cards featuring prominent Confederate military and political leaders. Though well received by the local Southern community, the loyalty of the Bendann's became suspect for the remainder of the war. An incident that occurred in their gallery in 1862 sheds light on the practice of photography during this era and points out the hazards faced by those working in a city under military rule.

Bendanns' wartime trademarks.

On the morning of June 30, U.S. Navy Lieutenant John Walters and his wife walked down Baltimore Street (the center of the city's photographic trade) seeking a studio to obtain a supply of photographs to distribute among their friends. The numerous galleries mixed in with the other retail stores along the avenue presented many with a difficult choice, but Mrs. Walters had been advised that the Bendanns did some of the best work in town. So at his wife's insistence, Lieutenant Walters accompanied her to the brothers' studio, although he reminded his wife of the rumors he had heard about the photographers' questionable loyalty.

The Walters entered the gallery's reception room and were greeted by David, the younger brother, who stood behind a wooden counter at the far end. Bendann described the studio's services to the couple who chose to have a dozen cartes de visite made. Lieutenant Walters wrote his name and rank in the company's ledger among those of previous customers. They were instructed to have a seat in the stylishly appointed waiting area until called for their sitting which was supposed to occur in about fifteen minutes.

While the couple awaited their turn, Bendann busied himself behind the counter. After fifteen minutes had passed, another pair entered the gallery and, to the surprise of the lieutenant and his wife, were immediately led upstairs to the studio for their sitting. The Walters became increasingly restless. Finally, at his wife's prodding, the officer approached the counter and asked David when they would be called for their appointment.

Though taken about ten years later, Baltimore Street had changed little since the day Lieutenant Walters and his wife had visited the Bendann gallery in the building immediately to the left of Gallagher's Mercantile College. Note the skylight on the roof. This image is reproduced from one side of a stereoview published by William M. Chase.

Bendann replied that things were now ready, but it was necessary for the lieutenant to first pay in advance for his order. The photographer explained that this practice was customary in New York and Boston for these types of photographs, and he further added that the firm had had problems with orders from officers that were never claimed. Walters was angry. He pointed out that he had signed the register with his name and rank and felt that Bendann was insulting his honor as an officer in the United States Navy. He added that this establishment was the last place he would go for a portrait since he usually had them done in New York or Philadelphia, but he only came there at his wife's insistence. The officer then threw his money on the counter adding that the brother had "a contemptible mode of doing business." With that, Bendann refused the money, declined to take the pictures, and ordered the couple from the building. Outraged, Walters leaned over the counter, struck the photographer in the face, and called him a "damned impertinent rebel."

David recoiled from the blow. Quickly, he opened a nearby desk drawer and grabbed a loaded revolver which he aimed at his attacker. The naval officer stepped back and drew his sword. The two men waited for the other to make the next deadly move. After several tense moments passed, Mrs. Walters finally ended the confrontation when she grabbed her husband's arm and pleaded with him to leave. Walters sheathed his weapon, but as he made his way out the door, he pledged to bring the provost marshal's (the military police) soldiers back to settle the affair. Bendann invited him to do so, and, as the couple departed, the gallery slipped into an uneasy silence.

Within the hour, soldiers arrived at the Bendann studio as promised. They placed David under arrest on charges of disloyalty and removed him to Fort McHenry for imprisonment. Over the next two months, all involved parties gave testimony about the incident and the character of the prisoner. It was decided that David would be released if he took an oath of allegiance to the United States. He refused, however, claiming that he was a citizen of Prussia and not the United States. The military command then moved him to a New York jail at Fort Lafayette and then to Fort Hamilton. Finally, his release was ordered on October 11, 1862, after more than three months of imprisonment. David had signed the oath of allegiance which included his vow "to in no wise aid or encourage the Rebels or so called Southern Confederacy." This brought an end to the incident, but not to the suspicions about the brothers' loyalty to the Union. Unlike other Northern cities, photography in Civil War Baltimore continued to have both political as well as commercial risks.

Once he reluctantly signed his oath of allegiance, David Bendann was finally released from prison over three months after his arrest. Private collection.

Portrait of the equipment and staff of army photographer Sam Cooley. Outdoor photography was particularly difficult during the Civil War years. National Archives.

OUTDOOR PHOTOGRAPHY

Many Civil War photographs that exist today were the product of thousands of photography studios that once dotted America's landscape. Some of the most memorable images, however, were not. The Civil War was not only the first war in history to produce such a vast visual record of participants, but it produced a remarkable collection of outdoor scenes - some of which have become permanent images in our collective national memory.

Photographers had to overcome many difficulties to preserve for posterity the scenes of their time. Because of the limitations of the collodion process, all cameramen had to operate close to a darkroom to sensitize and develop their fragile plates. Those who took their medium outdoors worked from a nearby "dark tent" or, more commonly, an enclosed compartment on the back of a wagon. A wagon could also be quickly moved to another location to record a new opportunity or to avoid the changing tide of the war. As in the studio, the amount of natural light, freshness of chemicals, temperature and humidity, and type of lens (landscape lenses allowed less light to enter the camera than those used in the studio) determined exposure times. Ten to fifteen seconds or more could be needed outdoors to sufficiently expose the plates. Consequently, no photographs of actual Civil War battles are known to have been made. Troops in combat were not going to stand still to be recorded by the photographer and his bulky equipment.

Outdoor photographs made during the Civil War generally fall into three categories. Those in the form of tintypes and ambrotypes are usually portraits of individuals or groups of soldiers. These were made by itinerant portrait photographers that always seemed to appear when Union troops camped. They were contracted and paid for by the subjects and were produced in limited number. The armies of both sides employed photographers as well. In addition to copying maps and plans, some were used to document railroad bridges, fortifications, and other works of military construction. The vast amount of outdoor views that we are most familiar with, however, were often produced for a different purpose.

The Civil War had created public demand for pictures of the places that filled the daily news. Since newspapers lacked the ability to photo-mechanically reproduce photographs, the public awaited the efforts of the adventurous photographer/entrepreneur who wanted to profit from this market. (*Harper's Weekly* and others sometimes copied photographs as woodcuts to print in their newspapers.) The ability to mass produce prints from a single glass negative seemed to promise financial reward to those who could overcome the expense and difficulty of operating in the field. And an earlier technical development helped to determine the format for many negatives used to make the photographs.

Even before the invention of photography, scientists had investigated the phenomenon of binocular vision that enables us to see in three-dimension. It was observed that each eye views a slightly different angle of the same scene, and the brain merges the two together to create the perception of depth. Experiments with photographs showed that this effect could also be duplicated and "stereography" or three-dimensional photography was born.

In stereography a photographer used a special camera with two lenses that approximated the spacing of human eyes. A scene was recorded on a single light sensitive plate by opening each of the lenses at the same time. This produced a pair of negatives with each slightly to the right or left of center. Contact prints were then made from the plate (as in the carte de visite) producing a pair of photographic prints. These were cut out and pasted to a rectangular card. When the card was viewed through a special viewer (which allowed each eye to only see one print from the pair), the brain merged the two together to produce the stereo or three-dimensional effect. Stereography quickly became a main attraction in parlor entertainment as the public clamored for the inexpensive "stereoview" cards that gave them a unique view of camps and battlefields.

Independent photographers and assistants soon took to the field to record the war. Several types of cameras, along with other photographic supplies, were carried in their specially adapted wagons that enabled them to make negatives for carte de visite, stereoview, and larger sized photographs. Mathew Brady's team eventually produced thousands of various size negatives of outdoor views. His photographers, led at one time by Alexander Gardner, were the first to ever record the grim scenes (taken at Antietam) of American soldiers killed in combat. "Let him who wishes to know what war is," wrote one reviewer, "look at this series of photographs."

Stereo negatives composed the bulk of the outdoor work taken for commercial publication. Of the plates exposed by Alexander Gardner (who had just left Brady's employment) and his team after the battle of Gettysburg, eighty percent were in the stereoview format.

Stereoview of the destruction caused when Confederate cavalry burned Chambersburg, Pennsylvania, in 1864. Publishers often copy one side of these cards for use as historical illustrations in books and magazines.

When seen through a special viewer, the brain merges the two images of a stereoview together to produce a three-dimensional effect.

Large view cameras were also part of these photographers' equipment. Designed for glass plates measuring 8 x 10 inches or more, they produced negatives that could be used to make larger albumen photographs. Prints were mounted on cardboard or paper to be sold individually or bound in books. In 1866, Gardner published his two volume *Sketch Book of the War* which contained 100 actual prints (approximately 7 x 9 inches) made from his wartime negatives. Each photograph was mounted on a separate page which included an accompanying description of the scene. These images along with the outdoor stereoviews, cartes de visite, and larger prints produced by Mathew Brady and others are the source for many Civil War photographs we recognize today.

"The Home of a Rebel Sharpshooter, Gettysburg," taken in Devil's Den on July 6, 1863 by cameraman Timothy O'Sullivan, was published by his employer, Alexander Gardner, from the stereo and 8 x 10 inch glass negatives that recorded the scene. Over a century later, photo-historian William Frassanito's landmark study of Gettysburg photographs (see "For More Information") discovered that the team of photographers had actually moved the body of the dead soldier about forty yards to compose this dramatic image. Library of Congress.

The negative for this print was taken by William Weaver in Baltimore, Maryland early in July 1861 after the arrest of the local police commissioners by the military command. Published later that month as a woodcut in Harper's Weekly, it is the only known photograph that shows soldiers in the streets of the city during the Civil War.

OCCUPATION OF MONUMENT SQUARE, BALTIMORE, MD., BY UNITED STATES ARTILLERY, BY ORDER OF MAJOR-GENERAL BANKS.—[PHOTOGRAPHED BY WEAVER.]

THE WARTIME EXPERIENCES OF A YOUNG PHOTOGRAPHER

The name "Bachrach" has been a hallmark for over 100 years denoting superior quality in the artistic and technical production of portrait photographs. America's "first family of photographers" still operates studios in New York, Boston, and three other cities where they serve their discriminating clientele. The founder of this enterprise was David Bachrach, Jr., one of the many forgotten photographers of the Civil War.

David was born in Hesse-Cassel, Germany, on July 16, 1845. He came to this country as a boy and received his education in the public schools of Hartford, Connecticut. After moving to Maryland, he began his career in photography at the age of 15 by working in the Baltimore Street studio of Robert Vinton Lansdale. After a year of apprenticeship, Bachrach entered the employment of William H. Weaver, an ornamental painter specializing in outdoor photography, who was occasionally employed by *Harper's Weekly*. By this time the Civil War was in progress, and Bachrach's association with Weaver gave the teenager a chance to view the war from a unique perspective.

On April 19, 1861, Baltimoreans attacked the Sixth Massachusetts Regiment as they passed through town on their way to defend the nation's capital. The incident sealed the fate of the city of divided loyalties. The troops returned a month later under the command of General Benjamin Butler and seized Federal Hill, which overlooked the harbor, during a fierce evening thunderstorm. Citizens awoke the following morning to the forces that directed their political actions for the remainder of the war. The Union Army had occupied Baltimore.

The rapidly developing events presented Weaver and his assistant with a photo-opportunity. The pair moved their cumbersome equipment to the top of Federal Hill in June to record the encampment which eventually became a heavily armed fort. *Harper's Weekly* published a woodcut copy of one of their photographs to let the nation see the "gentle but firm hand" that ruled the city. Several weeks later, the two recorded one of the most important local events.

The military command tightened a strong noose around Baltimore to ensure that the violence of the previous April would not be repeated. Arrests of newspaper editors, legislators, and other suspected disloyal citizens followed. During the first week of July, the decision was made to arrest the police commissioners. To prevent any further bloodshed, troops and cannon occupied strategic locations around the town where they remained encamped for a week. Weaver, accompanied by Bachrach, drove their darkroom wagon to Battle Monument Square on Calvert Street, a popular site for public gatherings, to record the scene. The resulting photograph, which *Harper's* also reproduced as a woodcut, is the only one yet discovered that shows troops in the streets of Baltimore during the Civil War.

Beginning in the spring of 1862, General George B. McClellan launched his Virginia Peninsula Campaign in an attempt to seize the Confederate capital at Richmond. Many ships carrying troops and supplies for the offensive, sailed from Baltimore's harbor down the Chesapeake Bay. Weaver recognized a chance to market his one dollar tintype portraits to the army gathering to the south, so he sent young Bachrach to investigate. The photographer's assistant traveled throughout the region experiencing firsthand the sights and the sounds of the conflict. When his employer concluded that the venture was too risky due to the uncertain fortunes of war, Bachrach returned to Baltimore. He traveled to Virginia again, however, several months later to work as an assistant to a photographer operating at Fort Gilmore (formerly the Confederate Fort Harrison) located about one mile from the James River.

While at Fort Gilmore, Bachrach helped his new employer record the faces of the soldiers in the area. When not working, his special status as the "daguerreotype man" got him permits to travel to the front lines. There he watched as pickets from both sides met and exchanged Lynchburg tobacco for coffee and Richmond newspapers for those from New York. One night, as the fort was bombarded by Confederate artillery, a general ordered him to remove a flag that flew above the photographer's tent since the commander was going to use it for his headquarters. Just as Bachrach was about to reach for it, a rebel shell took off the flagpole completely. That was the closest the young photographer had yet come to the realities of war.

In November 1863, David's photographic connection gave him another opportunity to witness history. A cameraman working for *Harper's* asked for Weaver's assistance in recording the dedication of the cemetery at Gettysburg, Pennsylvania. Bachrach drove the darkroom wagon for a day and a half over the Maryland hills by way of Westminster and Emmitsburg to his final destination. While Edward Everett delivered his one hour and a half speech, Bachrach did the technical work of photographing the crowd from a temporary stand about ninety feet from the podium. When Everett concluded, Abraham Lincoln rose to deliver his now famous address. Though it is unclear if Bachrach photographed the president during those brief moments, his 8 x 10

In September 1862, Weaver and Bachrach took a series of views of the cannon aimed at Baltimore from Fort Federal Hill. A gun crew from the 5th New York Heavy Artillery posed for the cameramen. Peale Museum.

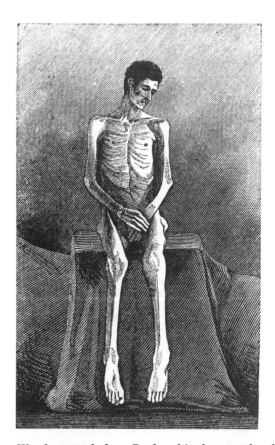
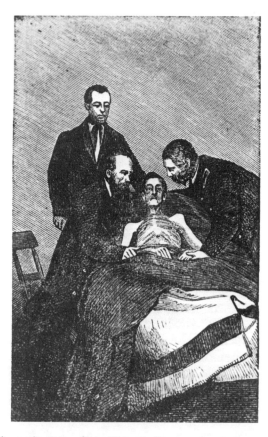

Woodcuts made from Bachrach's photographs of returning prisoners of war from Andersonville, Georgia.

inch wet-plate negatives made there were given to the photographer for *Harper's* who took the plates to the woodcut artists. (No views were later published credited to the plates and their fate is still unknown today.) Bachrach later noted that Lincoln's speech, which drew little response from the audience and the current newspapers, was "the greatest piece of English composition both in sentiment and composition, ever delivered."

Near the end of the war, Bachrach performed a duty that he considered to be the most important of his war experiences. After exchange, Union soldiers held in the notorious Confederate prison at Andersonville, Georgia, were returned to St. John's Hospital in Annapolis, Maryland. The surgeon-in-charge hired Bachrach to work for three months recording the condition of the cases brought there. Once he completed his assignment of photographing the soldiers, both dead and alive, David sent the negatives and prints to the surgeon-general's department. Later, some of his images brought him into direct conflict with one of the most powerful men of the time.

Shortly after the war, Andersonville's commandant, Henry Wirz, was put on trial for cruelty to prisoners. Newspapers published woodcuts of Bachrach's photographs that had been used as evidence against the defendant. Bachrach was indignant. Of the sixty cases that he had recorded, he recalled that each was officially reported as being caused by unrelated illness. He wrote a letter of protest to Secretary of War Stanton, and, when receiving no reply, paid a visit to his office to arrange a meeting. The photographer's request was denied, and it was intimated that he might receive a term in Old Capitol prison if he continued to persist. Bachrach appealed to General Winfield Hancock who finally obtained an audience with the Secretary of War for the young cameraman.

Bachrach was soon admitted to Stanton's office to state his case. The Secretary listened in silence as the photographer presented his objections over the use of his photographs. After he finished, Stanton stared at the young man. Then, in a harsh tone, he responded that he could not consider anyone justified in "giving aid and comfort to the enemy" after receiving pay from the government. Not to be intimidated, Bachrach retorted that he had completed all of the work contracted for and was under no obligation to have his photographs "used to misrepresent conditions." While glaring at his visitor, Stanton curtly replied, "In these times, you better keep quiet." With those words, Bachrach was abruptly dismissed.

David pondered his situation. Though willing to testify in the trial, he knew that suspicions of disloyalty could result in his arrest and imprisonment. Family and friends advised him to remain silent. Reluctantly, he finally heeded their advice. When Wirz was later convicted and sentenced to death, the young photographer felt that he could do no more. For the first time in history, photographs were possibly misused as evidence in court. As Bachrach went on to a distinguished career as owner of a chain of photography studios, the memories of his wartime experiences remained with him for the rest of his life.

Full plate tintype of the recreated Co. E, 2nd Maryland Infantry, C.S.A., taken on the 125th anniversary of the Battle of Antietam. The author is standing with arms folded on the left. Several photographers have revived the wet-plate process and some of their work could fool future collectors.

Confederate President Jefferson Davis is surrounded by his generals in this carte de visite of a larger lithographic print. The artist copied heads from photographs and created bodies and scenery to complete the montage. Though these types of pictures were often added to Civil War era albums, today's collectors usually prefer photographic portraits from life.

COLLECTORS' GUIDE

For those interested in the adventure and excitement of discovery and research, the collection of Civil War photographs can be a rewarding experience. The following hints will be helpful in guiding volunteers wanting to enlist in these growing ranks of collectors.

1. As a rule, original photographs of Confederate officers and enlisted men taken by Southern photographers are generally more valued than those of their Northern foes. Outdoor views by Southern photographers, particularly of Confederate units, camps, fortifications, and naval vessels, are rare and very desirable.

2. Weapons and equipment in a soldier's portrait, especially if they are uncommon, can enhance an image's value. Soldiers wearing unusual or rarely photographed uniforms are of interest, as are candid portraits that document aspects of the every day life of the soldier, such as cooking and entertainment. The subject's personal and unit identification included with a photograph also enhances its collectability. Caution should be taken, however, since some inscriptions have been added by fakers.

3. Previously unpublished or newly discovered images of prominent personalities of the period may command an extra premium. Bust portraits, unless they are identified or of someone famous, are usually less desirable since they offer little detail about uniforms and equipment. Generally, few collect military photographs just for their artistic or aesthetic merits alone.

4. Autographed photographs (usually cartes de visite) of prominent Civil War era personalities can be very valuable. Signatures on the fronts of cards are most desirable. Because of the possible monetary value, you should have reputable experts in Civil War autographs help determine authenticity.

5. Cartes de visite of prominent Civil War army officers published by E. & H. T. Anthony and C. D. Fredericks are collectible, but many were often published in large quantities, so few are rare and, consequently, do not command higher prices.

6. Outdoor scenes in tintypes and ambrotypes can be highly prized since they were usually not produced in large quantities. They give a rarer look outside the portrait photographer's tent.

7. The size of photographs can influence their market value. Collectors often place an added premium on interesting subject matter in cased images and paper prints that are larger than the sixth plate or carte de visite formats.

8. Stereoviews are collectible-particularly those of the more famous Civil War scenes such as Antietam and Gettysburg taken immediately after the battles. Views published by E. & H.T. Anthony and Alexander Gardner are popular. Any stereoview with the imprint of John C. Taylor or Taylor & Huntington, which used negatives made by Mathew Brady's company, were published after the war and bring lower prices today than those cards produced during the conflict.

9. Postwar portrait copies or enlargements of Civil War soldiers are not usually in great demand unless personal or unit identification further enhances their interest.

10. Photographs made from "life" (contact printed from or includes the original collodion plate) are more desirable than copies of an original either made during the period or later. (Cartes de visite of prominent personalities on cards that carry no photographer's imprint are probably pirated copies of images published by someone else.) Photographs of lithographic or engraved portraits usually have little interest among photography collectors. A carte de visite made from an actual negative that Abraham Lincoln sat for is far more desirable than the more common cartes copied from his widely circulated engraved portraits.

11. Care should be taken when purchasing photographs contained in miniature cases. Cartes de visite were usually not originally cased, although they are sometimes found that way. Postwar tintypes (often recognized by later-day clothing and studio props) have sometimes been placed in them giving the inaccurate impression

Cartes de visite of Lincoln engravings were very common during the Civil War era and receive little interest among serious collectors. Prints made directly from negatives taken from life are most desirable.

Inscribed carte de visite of W.S. Faulkner who served as an officer in the United States Colored Troops. Identified cartes of soldiers from important units can command a premium among collectors.

Gem tintype of Charles Collins from New York made by a special camera patented by Simon Wing in June 1862. Its movable lens made fifteen exposures on one 5 x 7 inch plate.

Bust portraits, such as this one of Nathaniel Matson, assistant surgeon with the First Connecticut Artillery, are usually less desirable among collectors unless identified.

of dating from the Civil War era. Also, images meant to be in miniature cases may have been removed from their original container and switched to another. Any identification included with it could then be misleading.

12. Because of the rising cost of collecting Civil War photographs, many collectors have specialized in specific regiments, states, personalities, and other themes. A collection of related images that illustrate the officers and enlisted men of a famous unit or those relating to a particular event are among the many ways a collector can create a focused collection.

13. Condition of photographs is an important consideration. Paper prints should not be torn, creased, or stained, and the image should show strong contrast between lights and darks. Ambrotypes should also be in high contrast, without cracking or flaking of emulsion. (Flaking of the dark backing may be repaired.) Tintypes should be free of rust and flaking emulsion as well. Of course there are always exceptions. Images of rarity and historic importance can still be valuable in spite of condition problems.

14. There are a few photographers today that have revived the old processes of making ambrotypes and tintypes. New images made of Civil War reenactors could possibly fool a novice. In addition, cartes de visite have been faked and/or spurious identifications have been added. Until you feel confident in recognizing these, seek the advise of reputable dealers in Civil War photography who guarantee their merchandise.

15. Along with the joys of collecting comes the added responsibility of caring for these artifacts. No photographs should ever be displayed in direct sunlight. Special plastic sleeves, available in various sizes, can be purchased to protect paper images during storage and handling. Storage boxes and folders made of "acid free" paper should be used as well. (Ask museum curators or photography dealers for sources for these materials.) Wooden backings of wall frames must be removed immediately since the acidity of the wood causes the discoloration and eventual deterioration of paper. A stable environment of moderate temperature (70 to 75 degrees) and relative humidity (about 50%) is also good for your collection.

As with any collecting field, the more you know, the better you can be at investing time and money. Read the resources listed here in "For More Information." Attend Civil War relic and collectors' shows to learn market values and meet the experts in the field. And, most importantly, have fun in this great adventure searching antique shows and shops, auctions, and flea markets for these unique images of America's past.

FOR MORE INFORMATION

The following is a recommended list of resources for those who would like to learn more about Civil War photography. Most can be obtained from Civil War book dealers.

Albaugh, William A. *Confederate Faces*. Solana Beach, Ca.: Verde Publishers, 1970.
    More Confederate Faces. Washington, D.C.: Wm. A. Albaugh, 1972.

William Albaugh was a pioneer in the collecting and study of Confederate relics. In these two books, he published a comprehensive catalogue of period images of Confederate officers and enlisted men. Though long out of print, they are often cited as a reference for Southern photographs on the market today.

Coates, Earl J. and Thomas, Dean S. *Introduction to Civil War Small Arms*. Gettysburg, Pa.: Thomas Publications, 1990.

Eventually image collectors are going to need a guide that will help them identify the firearms that appear in Civil War photographs. This book illustrates and discusses the various types of rifles, muskets, and handguns used during the conflict and reproduces period images of soldiers posed with one. Other useful information is also included.

Confederate Calendar Works, P.O. Drawer 2084, Austin, Texas 78768. Write for current price.

This company publishes a yearly calendar that illustrates each month with an image and biography of a Confederate soldier. It remains a valuable reference long after the calendar is out of date.

Darrah, William C. *The World of Stereographs*. Gettysburg, Pa.: W.C. Darrah, 1977.
    Cartes de Visite in Nineteenth Century Photography. Gettysburg, Pa.: W.C. Darrah, 1981.

Darrah was a pioneer in the collection and research of stereographs and cartes de visite. His works are the basic guidebooks for those working with these particular photographic formats.

Davis, William C. *The Image of War 1861-1865*. 4 vols. Garden City, New York: Doubleday & Co., Inc. 1981.
    Touched by Fire: A Photographic Portrait of the Civil War. 2 vols. Boston, Mass.:
    Little, Brown & Co., 1985.

These books follow in the tradition of Francis Miller's work by compiling previously unpublished Civil War photographs. The high quality of photographic reproduction and informative text make them an invaluable resource.

Frassanito, William. *Gettysburg - A Journey in Time*. New York: Charles Scribner's Sons, 1975.
    Antietam - The Photographic Legacy of America's Bloodiest Day. New York:
    Charles Scribner's Sons, 1978.
    Grant and Lee: The Virginia Campaigns, 1864-1865. New York:
    Charles Scribner's Sons, 1983.

Frassanito researched all of the period photographs taken at these Civil War battlefields and determined exactly where most were taken. These pioneering books corrected inaccuracies and made new discoveries which have led to renewed study of the photographs of this era.

Gardner, Alexander. *Gardner's Sketch Book of the Civil War*. New York: Dover Publications, Inc., 1959.

This is a reprint of the two volume book, published by Gardner in 1866, that contained 100 prints from his wartime negatives. Many of the most familiar images of the Civil War are found among these pages.

Hunt, Roger D. and Brown, Jack R. *Brevet Brigadier Generals in Blue*. Gaithersburg, Maryland:
    Olde Soldier Books, Inc. 1990.

Following in the tradition of Ezra Warner's *Generals in Blue*, this book lists alphabetically the 1,400 brevet generals of the Union army during the Civil War. Included are biographical information, service records, and portrait photographs. It is an important aid for identifying images.

Kelbaugh, Ross J. *Directory of Civil War Photographers*. Baltimore: Historic Graphics, 1990.

This multi-volume series uses city directories and the Internal Revenue Assessment Lists to document the locations and dates of operation for professional photographers throughout the United States. It is a standard reference for dating Civil War era photographs signed by their maker. Contact Thomas Publications for a list of current volumes that are available.

    Directory of Maryland Photographers, 1839-1900. Baltimore: Historic Graphics, 1988.

Few state directories for photographers exist covering the Civil War years. Ones that place them at a specific location within a certain time frame are most useful. This reference helps in dating photographs signed by photographers that worked in Maryland during the nineteenth century. Included are studio addresses and dates of occupancy, as well as biographies and portraits of some of the more prominent.

Miller, Francis T. *Photographic History of the Civil War.* 10 Vols. New York: The Review of Reviews Co.
1912; reprint ed., Secaucus, New Jersey: Blue & Frey Press, 1987.

Miller's ten volume study was the first major work to chronicle the story of the Civil War through photographs. It still remains an important tool for those researching this era and is available in reprint.

Military Images Magazine, RD 1, Box 99A, Henryville, PA 18332. Write for current subscription rate.

The Civil War is the general focus of this bimonthly magazine devoted to the indepth study of soldiers' uniforms, equipment, and fighting organizations as told through photographs.

Taft, Robert. *Photography and the American Scene.* New York: Dover Publications, 1964.

This classic, first published in 1938, and now available in reprint, chronicles the development of photography in America during the nineteenth century. It remains a standard reference in the field.

Turner, William A. *Even More Confederate Faces.* Orange, Virginia: Moss Publications, 1983.

Following the tradition of William Albaugh, Turner's book presents additional photographs of Confederate officers and enlisted men and is invaluable for Confederate image collectors.

Warner, Ezra J. *Generals in Gray: Lives of the Confederate Commanders.* Baton Rouge, La.:
Louisiana State University Press, 1959.
Generals in Blue: Lives of the Union Commanders. Baton Route, La.:
Louisiana State University Press, 1964.

Collectors of Civil War photography will eventually need a resource to help identify subjects in images. These books contain short biographies and portraits of Union and Confederate generals and are helpful for conducting this kind of research.

Welling, William. *Photography in America: The Formative Years, 1839-1900.* New York: Thomas Y. Crowell Co., 1978.

Welling gives a year by year account of the history of photography in America from its beginnings through the end of the nineteenth century. It included many illustrations.

WHERE TO SEE CIVIL WAR PHOTOGRAPHS

The following institutions have major collections of Civil War photographs. State and local historical societies may also have images from this period as well. Check with the curator of prints and photographs for the organization in your area.

Library of Congress
Prints and Photographs Division
James Madison Memorial Building, Room 337
First Street and Independence Ave., SE Washington, D.C. 20540

The division houses thousands of original Civil War photographs in all formats including one set of Mathew Brady's negatives and the Brady-Handy Collection. Researchers can be admitted during regular weekday hours to study images. Copies can be ordered at reasonable cost.

Massachusetts Commandery of the Military Order of the Loyal Legion of the United States Collection (Mollus Collection)
U.S. Army Military History Institute
Carlisle Barracks, Pennsylvania 17013

This collection contains over 40,000 images taken during the Civil War of which three quarters are soldiers' portraits. The institute has expanded it through their project to copy photographs of all who served in the North and South. Over 80,000 have been amassed of which 90 percent are Union soldiers. The collection is cross-catalogued and reproductions can be ordered for a nominal fee.

National Archives
Eighth and Pennsylvania Avenue, NW
Washington, D.C. 20408

The Mathew Brady Collection of Civil War Photographs (Record Group 111), produced from a second group of Brady's negatives, is available on microfilm for viewing in Room 400. Copies or photographs can be ordered from the National Archives for a nominal cost.

GLOSSARY

albumen paper - photographic paper most commonly used for printing Civil War era photographs from glass negatives. Made from paper coated with chicken egg albumen and common salt which was rendered light sensitive by floating in a solution of silver nitrate. It is usually recognized by its glossy finish.

ambrotype - a variation of the collodion process which produced a photographic negative on glass that turned into a positive when backed with black material.

bust portrait - view of the subject's head, shoulders, and upper part of the chest only. These types of portraits are usually less desirable among Civil War collectors.

carte de visite (visiting card) - photographs printed from a glass negative and mounted on a 2 1/2 by 4 inch card. Often called "CDV's" by collectors, these are common photographic formats for Civil War era portraits.

cased or "hard" image - general names sometimes used by collectors to describe daguerreotypes, ambrotypes, and tintypes that were placed in a miniature case.

collodion - the sticky transparent solution that holds light sensitive chemicals on glass. This was the key ingredient for all Civil War photography.

daguerreotype - the earliest, widely practiced form of photography that used polished silver plates as the base for the image. Few daguerreotypes were taken during the Civil War.

fixed - chemical treatment used to make photographic plates and paper insensitive to light.

gem pictures - small tintype or albumen pictures about 1 inch by 1 inch or smaller which were placed on or in carte de visite size mounts. They sold for as little as 25 cents for four and were most common during the last years of the war.

gutta-purcha case - name sometimes used to describe thermoplastic "Union" cases used to hold ambrotypes and tintypes. Gutta-purcha, a natural substance, was actually not used in the manufacturing of these cases.

mat - decorative sheet of brass placed between the image plate and cover glass of a cased image.

miniature case - general name for all cases used to house daguerreotypes, ambrotypes, and some tintypes. This was originally used to describe the cases that held small painted portraits popular before the invention of photography.

negative - the reverse of the light and shade found on a photograph. In collodion photography, this effect is produced chemically on a glass plate from which the positive photograph is made.

portrait from life - portrait produced on or from the actual collodion plate that the photographer exposed in the camera during the subject's sitting.

preserver - decorative brass edging that held together the sandwich of image plate, mat, and cover glass of a cased image.

salt print - photographic paper first treated with a salt solution before being sensitized. Prints from this process, which lack the gloss of albumen paper, are found most often among early war images.

solar camera enlarger - apparatus invented before the Civil War that enabled photographers to make photographic enlargements from glass negatives. Prints usually had to be hand colored to achieve satisfactory results.

stereograph, stereoview, stereocard - rectangular cards on which are mounted two views of the same subject. When seen through a special viewer, a three-dimensional effect is produced.

tintype - name commonly used today for collodion photographs made on blackened sheet iron although tin was never used in the process. Photographers during the Civil War called these images melainotypes or ferrotypes.

vignetted - technique where the photographer shaded off the edges of the background behind the subject. This is most often found on carte de visite bust portraits.

wet-plate process - another name for the photographic process which used collodion to hold light sensitive chemicals to glass. Plates had to be exposed and developed while still "wet" or tacky.

woodcut - photographs reproduced in Civil War newspapers were copied by artists on to wood blocks where they were cut out in relief for printing.